A DIALOGUE ON
G. E. MOORE'S
ETHICAL PHILOSOPHY

A DIALOGUE ON
G. E. MOORE'S
ETHICAL PHILOSOPHY

TOGETHER WITH AN ACCOUNT OF THREE TALKS WITH
G. E. MOORE ON DIVERSE PHILOSOPHICAL QUESTIONS

BY

CONSTANTINE CAVARNOS

INSTITUTE FOR BYZANTINE
AND MODERN GREEK STUDIES
115 Gilbert Road
Belmont, Massachusetts 02178
U.S.A.

PREFACE

The *Dialogue* is a discussion of the ethical philosophy of the very influential English philosopher George Edward Moore (1873-1958), as contained in his magnum opus *Principia Ethica*. It seeks to point out and clarify some basic ideas contained in the *Principia* by posing and answering certain questions, commenting on Moore's views, and comparing them with those of two other eminent English philosophers, contemporaries of his, C. D. Broad and W. D. Ross, who participate in the dialogue.

Written many years ago, this work is published now 'for the first time. It is addressed to all those who are interested in the ethical philosophy of G. E. Moore, in his analytical approach to philosophical questions, of which this dialogue affords illustrations, and more widely to those who are interested in the clarification of basic ethical notions and wonder about the possibility of achieving unity and system in ethics.

The *Three Talks with G. E. Moore* that follow the *Dialogue* took place in the winter of 1947-1948 at Moore's home in Cambridge, England. I was a Sheldon Traveling Fellow in Philosophy at the time, meeting and conferring with the philosophers there, including Moore, C. D. Broad, Bertrand Russell, A. C. Ewing, R. B. Braithwaite, and J. O. Wisdom, attending some of their lectures, and working on my Ph.D. dissertation, *The Classical Theory of Relations*. The account of these talks, which appears in print for the first time, is the record of them that I kept in my Diary. I have omitted items which I thought would not be of wider interest, but have added nothing, except two quotations from Moore's writings and the notes at the end.

Being a record of meetings and discussions that actually took place, the *Three Talks* constitute an addition to the primary sources for the study of the thought and character of G. E. Moore. Also, they should be of interest for whatever light they throw on the diverse philosophical questions that are raised and answered.

CONSTANTINE CAVARNOS

Belmont, Massachusetts
January, 1979

CONTENTS

A DIALOGUE ON
G. E. MOORE'S
ETHICAL PHILOSOPHY

A DIALOGUE ON
G. E. MOORE'S ETHICAL PHILOSOPHY

PERSONS OF THE DIALOGUE

PHILAGATHOS, *who leads*　　　G. E. MOORE
　　the discussion

C. D. BROAD　　　　　　　　W. D. ROSS

PHILAGATHOS.[1]　How fortunate I am to meet on one and the same occasion three so distinguished ethicists as you Moore, and you Broad, and you Ross! And at a time when my mind is very confused on the subject of ethics, from my having read many ethical treatises recently, but reflected so little upon them. There is a saying, as you know, that when the disciple is ready the master will appear. And lo! scarcely have I prepared myself and not one, but three masters have appeared.

MOORE.　I am glad to see that you have such confidence in us, young Philagathos, and I hope that we may prove of some help to you. However, I must say at once that the subject-matter of ethics not only seems to be, but actually is, inherently one of great complexity; and I disavow any compelling interest in unity and system. Moreover, I must point out that my views and those of Broad and Ross are not exactly alike; that, in-

11

deed, they sometimes differ significantly. Hence you must not expect all your confusions to be cleared up in this discussion. However, I promise you this much: that you will learn what the main sources of the difficulties and disagreements in ethics are; and that many of your ethical notions will become clearer. But tell us, what ethical philosophers have you read?

PHIL.   I have read all the ancient Greeks, many Westerners, and some Orientals. Also, I have read some histories of Western ethical philosophy.

MOORE.   I see. I suppose then you have read, or read about, Henry Sidgwick and Franz Brentano?

PHIL.   Yes, I have.

MOORE.   Good! For of all moral philosophers Sidgwick and Brentano have most eminently avoided certain fundamental confusions and fallacies. And as their doctrines are in very important ways similar to mine, you will have little difficulty following me.

PHIL.   I sincerely hope so. But tell me, what have been the basic errors of nearly all moral philosophers of the past?

MOORE.   "It seems to me that in ethics, as in all other philosophical studies, the difficulties and disagreements are mainly due to a very simple cause: namely, to the attempt to answer questions, without first discovering precisely *what* question it is which you desire to answer." Now there are two kinds of question which "moral philosophers have always professed to answer, but which they almost always confused *both with one another, and with other questions.*"

PHIL.   What are these two kinds of question?

MOORE.   They are, first: "What kind of *things* ought

to exist for their own sakes," that is, "are good in themselves," or "have *intrinsic* value? Second: "What kind of *actions* ought we to perform?" That is, "What is 'right action' or 'duty?'" Once we see clearly the nature of these two questions, a *third* one arises: "What is the nature of the *evidence* by which alone any ethical proposition can be proved or disproved, confirmed or rendered doubtful?" Nearly all moral philosophers have not only confused these questions with one another and with other questions, but have either tried to offer evidence for propositions pertaining to them for which *no* evidence *whatever* can be adduced, or have failed to adduce the *right* kind of evidence for propositions where evidence *can* be adduced and is necessary. I think that ethical discussion hitherto has consisted chiefly in reasoning of this totally irrelevant kind.

PHIL.   In other words, it has consisted chiefly in the fallacy of *'ignoratio elenchi.'*

MOORE.   Yes. That is just the name for it, though this term is commonly used to refer to the sophistical use of the fallacy, and it would not be right for us to identify the greater number of philosophers with sophists. They committed the fallacy quite unwittingly. Wouldn't you agree?

PHIL.   I agree, without hesitation. But now I have a further question. What, to your mind, is the subject-matter of ethics?

MOORE.   The science of ethics "investigates assertions about that property of things which is denoted by the term 'good' and the converse property denoted by the term 'bad.'" "Ethics must enquire not only what things are universally related to goodness, but also, what this predicate (goodness or good), to which they are related, is."

PHIL.   I understand. Ethics, for you, is the science which is concerned with the meaning of moral predicates and with the investigation of assertions involving them.

MOORE.   That is correct

PHIL.   You stand, then, in marked contrast with men like Durkheim and Lévy-Bruhl, who seek "to replace moral philosophy by the 'science des moeurs,' the historical and comparative study of the moral beliefs and practices of mankind."[2]

MOORE.   Indeed.

PHIL.   Again, your conception of ethics marks you off from those who hold that ethics is a 'normative' science, either in the sense of (a) propaganda or hortatory discourse, or (b) edification, or (c) application or guidance, or (d) expressive discourse, or (e) systematic normative ethics.

MOORE.   Definitely.

PHIL.   Now do you Broad, and you, Ross agree with Moore's conception of moral philosophy.

BROAD.   I certainly do. I think that the first and most fundamental problem of pure ethics is to examine the various *ethical characteristics* denoted by the words 'good' and 'bad,' 'right' and 'wrong,' 'ought' and 'duty,' and synonyms of these words; and to determine whether these characteristics are unique and peculiar — that is, whether they cannot be analyzed without remainder in terms of non-ethical characteristics.

ROSS.   I, too, accept this conception of ethics.

PHIL.   Fine. Let us suppose, now, that a moral philosopher goes about this task and comes out with the conclusion that some or all the 'moral predicates' or 'ethical characteris-

tics' cannot be analyzed, or cannot be analyzed without remainder, in terms of non-ethical characteristics. What kind
of ethical theory shall we say he is developing?

BROAD.   A 'non-naturalistic' theory.

PHIL.   And suppose another moral philosopher comes
out with the opposite conclusion, namely, that *all* ethical characteristics *can* be analyzed in terms of non-ethical characteristics. We shall call this 'naturalistic?'

BROAD.   Yes.

PHIL.   And I reckon that non-naturalistic theories will
take different forms, according to what ethical characteristics
have been found to be irreducible; while naturalistic theories
will take various forms according to what non-ethical characteristics have been supposed to constitute the complete
analysis of ethical characteristics.

BROAD.   Exactly.

PHIL.   From what you said about the subject-matter of
ethics, Moore, I got the impression that you believe that the
fundamental, irreducible, concept of ethics is the one you
denote by 'good' or 'goodness.' I wonder if I am right.

MOORE.   You are quite right.

PHIL.   Is your position the same on this point, Ross?

ROSS.   No. I agree with Moore that 'goodness' is an
irreducible quality, but I find 'rightness' irreducible, too.

PHIL.   And what is your view on this point, Broad?

BROAD.   I am inclined to agree with Ross. It seems
almost certain to me that 'right' and 'ought' cannot be defined
in terms of 'good,' which itself, I believe, is irreducible.

PHIL. You and Ross are, then, the very antithesis of 'naturalism.'

BROAD. Yes. I think that no form of ethical natural-ism is in the least plausible, except the 'psychological' form, the sort of theory that David Hume developed. This theory attempts to define ethical characteristics, such as 'good' and 'right,' in terms of characteristics such as pleasantness and ap-proval. But I do not know of any definition of ethical con-cepts in purely psychological terms which seems to me to be satisfactory. Therefore, I think it very likely, though not ab-solutely certain, that ethical naturalism is false, and that all ethical characteristics are *sui generis.*

PHIL. I see. Now let us go back to the predicate 'good.' I hope I shall be able to learn something definite about it. I understand, Moore, that you have made some statements about 'good' which have caused quite a stir among ethicists; and I would like to hear exactly what was the view you put forth.

MOORE. The view I have expounded about the pre-dicate 'good' or 'goodness' is simply this. The predicate 'good' denotes *one unique simple* object of thought among innumer-able others. It is simple, without parts, or unanalyzable, and therefore *indefinable.* For we define a thing (in the truest sense of the word 'define') by analyzing it into its constituent parts; and if a thing cannot be so analyzed, that is, if it is not complex but simple, it cannot be defined.[3]

PHIL. But suppose someone were to ask you: "Mr. Moore, *what* is 'good?'" What would your answer be?

MOORE. My answer would be that good is good; and that would be the end of the matter.

PHIL.   But if he were a persistent fellow, and pressed you for an example of another notion which is simple and indefinable, what would you say?

MOORE.   I would give him the example of 'yellow.' Good is a simple notion just as yellow is a simple notion. And just as you cannot by any manner of means explain to any one who does not already know it, what yellow is, so you cannot explain what good is.

PHIL.   But all this seems to imply that nearly all moral philosophers, in attempting to define 'good,' have committed a fallacy, and a very serious one.

MOORE.   That is exactly the point I make. Almost all moral philosophers have gone astray at the very outset of their enquiry; for almost all have tried to define 'good.' In so doing they virtually said that "good is not good but is something else!" This I have called 'the naturalistic fallacy.' It is time for ethicists to free themselves from it, and to take as their motto Butler's saying that "Everything is what it is and not another thing." The 'naturalistic fallacy' reduces what is used as a fundamental principle of ethics either (1) to a tautology, or (2) to a statement about the meaning of a word. Thus, we are sometimes told that "good is pleasure," or "good is that which is desired." What happens here is that good is defined as something else. And it is then impossible either to deny such a definition or to prove that any other definition is wrong; for nominal definitions cannot be questioned or disproved. The other alternative is that the discussion is after all a verbal one. That is, when A says that "Good means pleasant," and B says that "Good means desired," they may merely wish to assert that *most people* have used the word for what is pleasant and for what is desired, respectively. But hardly either of these discussions is ethics.

PHIL.   I see your point quite clearly. Yet here is a difficulty that at once presents itself to me. 'Good' is like yellow, unanalyzable and therefore indefinable. Yet it seems possible to give a real definition of 'yellow.' Thus, we can say that yellow is a color, and that it comes between red and green in the scale of pure color qualities. Now while I do not believe that ethical relativism is a sound view, I think that this comparison may cause the relativist to say to you: "If 'yellow' can be defined in such a way, why cannot we similarly connect 'good' with conation? I can define 'good' as 'the object of any desire or interest.'"

MOORE.   The answer to this, dear Philagathos, has already been given: Good is good and not something else.[4] But as regards my comparison of 'good' with 'yellow,' I admit it was not an apt one.

ROSS.   The ethical relativist, Philagathos, may also be silenced by advancing certain other considerations. Thus, "when we call something good we are thinking of it as possessing in itself a certain attribute and are not thinking of it as necessarily having an interest taken in it." Do you agree?

PHIL.   I do.

ROSS.   Again, is it not evident that it is "possible to think that some of the things in which an interest has been taken have nevertheless been bad?"

PHIL.   Certainly.

ROSS.   "But if 'good' and 'object of interest' meant exactly the same, it would be impossible to think either of these two things which it clearly is possible to think."

PHIL.   Absolutely.

ROSS. Now if this is the case, the view that 'good' and 'object of interest' stand for the same notion must maintain, if it is to be plausible, something quite different; what it really must maintain is that "whereas most people think that certain things have a characteristic, goodness, distinct from that of being objects of interest, nothing has any such characteristic."

PHIL. That seems to be the only thing it could really mean.

ROSS. "Then the question arises, what could have led mankind to form this quite superfluous notion to which nothing in reality corresponds? It is *not* as if the notion of goodness were a *complex* notion, formed, like such notions as that of 'centaur,' by a play of fancy in which characteristics found separate in reality are imagined to coexist; for there are no characteristics of which 'good' can be said to be a compound." Not only may we ask how the notion of 'good' could have come into being if it were not the apprehension of a reality, but we may also claim *that we are directly aware* that certain actions, such as those which manifest conscientiousness, have a value of their own, not identical with or even dependent upon our or any else's taking an interest in them. I submit that *reason* informs us of this as surely as it informs us of anything, and that to distrust reason here is in principle to distrust its power of ever knowing reality.

PHIL. Excellent, all that you have said. But there remains an apparent difficulty common to the position taken by you, Moore, and Broad. All three of you are in accord that the notion 'good' is unanalyzable. Yet it seems that the ingredients of the physical world are analyzable without limit. Now if 'goodness' is unanalyzable, then we are involved in the "assumption that the quality in question does not belong to the physical world."[5]

MOORE. But this I grant; for assert that the predicate 'good' denotes a 'non-natural' quality. And I see no difficulty inherent in this view.

PHIL. Possibly there is none. But I am not sure that I understand your meaning when you say that 'good' is a 'non-natural' quality. Exactly what do you mean by 'non-natural' as distinct from 'natural?'

MOORE. By a 'natural *object*' I mean any object that is capable of existing in time. For instance, a stone, a mind, an explosion, an experience, and so on. All natural objects have natural characteristics or qualities, and some natural objects have also 'non-natural' characteristics. Each *natural* characteristic of a natural object could be conceived as existing *in time all by itself,* and every natural object is a whole whose parts are its natural characteristics, whereas a 'non-natural' characteristic of a natural object is one which *cannot* be conceived as existing in time all by itself, but only as the property of some natural object.

PHIL. But it seems to me that *every* characteristic that you would call natural as well as every characteristic that you would call non-natural satisfies your criterion of non-naturalness. For, as Aristotle points out, we do not find characteristics, such as colors, shapes, sizes, and so on, existing loose, but always existing in something, always as parts or aspects of something. Hence, in this sense no characteristic could be natural. For instance, I cannot conceive the shape or color of an apple as existing in time all by themselves. Accordingly, on this account, it would seem that these characteristics are non-natural. Yet, you regard these as natural characteristics.

MOORE. I see, Philagathos, that I haven't made my meaning clear. The distinction between natural and non-natural characteristics is very difficult to explain.[6] But our friend Broad is in readiness to speak. Let us listen to what he has to say.

BROAD. I think I know what you are really intending to say, Moore. A 'natural' characteristic is "any characteristic which either (1) we become aware of by inspecting our sense-data or introspecting our experience, or (2) is definable wholly in terms of characteristics of the former kind together with the notions of cause and substance." Thus 'yellowness,' and psychological characteristics, such as the 'fear-quality' and the 'anger-quality,' etc. are natural characteristics. A 'non-natural' characteristic, on the other hand, can be described epistemologically in negative terms as follows: (1) no one could become aware of it by inspecting his sense-data or introspecting his experiences, and (2) it is not definable in terms of characteristics of which one could be aware in those ways together with the notions of cause and substance.

MOORE. That is my meaning.

PHIL. I find this distinction helpful. But the question now arises in my mind: Granting that 'goodness' is a name for a non-natural characteristic, how do we become aware of it — how do we know it? Obviously, the comparison of 'good' with yellow does not help us here, but can only confuse us. For yellow is a natural characteristic of which we become aware by inspecting our sense-data; while of 'good' no one become aware by inspecting his sense-data, since it is a non-natural characteristic: none of our senses reveals to us the characteristic 'good.'

BROAD.   Quite right. And I think that it is equally clear that "no simple psychological characteristic, such as we could discover by introspecting our experiences, can be identified with goodness." By introspecting we do not become aware of 'goodness,' but only of "experiences which are pleasant or unpleasant, toned with desire or with aversion, fearful, hopeful, and so on."

PHIL.   How, then, do we become aware of goodness?

BROAD.   By *reason*. "If goodness be a non-natural characteristic, then anyone's idea of it must be an *a priori* notion, or contain *a priori* notions as elements" (supposing it is a complex non-natural characteristic). "For an *a priori* notion just is an idea of a characteristic which is *not* manifested to us *in sensation or introspection* and is not definable wholly in terms of characteristics which are so manifested."

PHIL.   I am inclined to agree with you that goodness is apprehended by reason, and is an *a priori* notion. From certain statements you made sometime back, Ross, I would say that you are in perfect agreement with Broad on these points. Am I right?

ROSS.   Yes.

PHIL.   How about you, Moore? What is your view?

MOORE.   I do not commit myself to any explanation as to *how* we become aware of the characteristic 'good.' *That* we become aware of it is a fact. *How* we become aware of it is another question, an answer to which I am not ready to give.[7]

PHIL.   Very well. Let us now take up the question

regarding the *definability* of 'goodness.' Would you, Broad, agree with Moore and Ross that it is indefinable? Although I cannot at the moment think of any definition of it, still I feel that some definition should be possible.

BROAD.   I am afraid I cannot agree with Moore and Ross. It seems to me that a definition of 'goodness' in apparently non-natural terms is possible. Thus, "it would not be implausible to suggest that 'x is intrinsically good' means that 'x is something which it would be *right* or *fitting* to desire as an end.' " Here 'right' or 'fitting' seem to be non-natural characteristics.

PHIL.   What you say is very much to my mind. But supposing 'goodness' is utterly indefinable, as you Moore and Ross maintain. It would seem to be impossible to make any statements involving the notion 'good.'

MOORE.   That by no means follows. Indeed, I believe that there are countless meaningful statements which can be made involving this notion. Thus, there is much that I can say about the nature of the chief *objects* to which the term 'good' can be strictly applied. Hence, while 'good' is indefinable, it is quite possible to give an account of *'the* good.'

PHIL.   Would you please illustrate?

MOORE.   Gladly. In a discussion about 'the good,' that is, about the *things* that are good, one must be careful to distinguish between means and ends, between what is 'good as a means' and what is 'good as an end,' between the 'extrinsically good' and the 'intrinsically good.' Ethicists in the past have not always made this distinction as clearly as they might have. Now judgments of the form 'x is intrinsically good,' or what is the same thing, 'x ought to exist for its own sake,' are (1) synthetic, (2) intuitive, and (3) logically independent of all judgments of existence, natural or metaphysical.

PHIL.   I understand. And as regards such judgments, are you a rationalist?

MOORE.   I am not prepared to say that. When I say that such propositions are 'intuitions' I mean merely to assert that they are incapable of proof; I imply nothing whatever as to the manner or origin of our cognition of them. That is, I mean only that with regard to these propositions no relevant evidence whatever can be adduced: from no other truth, except themselves alone, can it be inferred that they are either true or false.

PHIL.   I see. Now what exactly is *your* stand on this matter, Ross?

ROSS.   I agree with Moore insofar as he holds that such judgments are intuited; but I go beyond him and maintain that not only such judgments, but our 'prima facie' duties *also* are intuited and, further, that they are intuited by reason. In ethics, "we have no more direct way of access to the facts about rightness and goodness and about what things are right or good, than by *thinking* about them. . . ." Now "the moral convictions of thoughtful and well-educated people are the data of ethics, just as sense-perceptions are the data of a natural science. Just as some of the latter have to be rejected as illusory, so have some of the former; but as the latter are rejected only when they are in conflict with other more accurate sense-perceptions, the former are rejected only when they are in conflict with other convictions which stand better the test of reflection."

PHIL.   Would you say that these convictions are know-ledge? That hardly seems to be the case, for knowledge is stable, and a true proposition never becomes absolete and can never be found to be inconsistent with another true proposition.

ROSS.   I maintain that what we are apt to describe as 'what we think' about moral questions contains a considerable amount that we do not merely think but really know, and that this forms the standard by reference to which the truth of any moral theory has to be tested.

PHIL.   Your view has considerable similarity to Moore's, except that you are explicit as to the manner of cognition, and that you broaden the extent of our intuitive knowledge. Now I would like to see with whom Broad sides on this issue, or what position he takes.

BROAD.   I am inclined to agree here with Ross. I think that there are *necessary* propositions connecting ethical char-acteristics — both concepts of value, such as 'good,' 'bad,' 'merit,' and so on, and concepts of obligation, such as 'right' and 'duty' — with non-ethical characteristics; and that these propositions can be seen to be necessary by *inspection.*

PHIL.   You mean these propositions are *synthetic a priori?*

BROAD.   Yes. And it seems to me that if this is the case the most plausible supposition is that they are reached by 'intuitive induction.' After observing a number of instances of an ethical characteristic being always the same, we see (or think we see) a necessary connection.

PHIL.   The views of all three of you are in substantial agreement. But which of them best lays hold of the truth

I am at the moment unable to tell. Let us, however, leave aside this epistemological discussion for the present and consider what things are good. For if good things are really good, one must make no delay, but seek to track them down with all possible haste. Moore, since you are a veteran in the chase, won't you make the start?

MOORE.   Very gladly, Philagathos. I commence by saying this: When we try to answer the question what things are good in themselves, we must observe two principles. First, "it is necessary to consider what things are such that, if they existed *by themselves,* in absolute isolation, we should yet judge their existence to be good." And second, "the intrinsic value of *a whole* is *neither identical with nor proportional to* the sum of the values of its parts." The first may be called 'the principle of isolation;' the second, 'the principle of organic unities.' Now the predicates good and bad apply to a multiplicity of things. "There is *a vast variety* of great *intrinsic goods* and great *intrinsic evils.*" Personal affections and aesthetic enjoyments include all the greatest, and by far the greatest, goods we can imagine. The simplest of these are highly complex wholes, composed of parts which have little or no value in themselves. They all involve (1) consciousness of an object, and almost all involve (2) an emotional attitude towards this object. "But though they thus have certain characteristics in common, the vast majority of qualities in respect of which they differ from one another are equally essential to their value: neither the generic character of all, nor the specific character of each, is either greatly good or greatly evil by itself; they owe their value, or demerit, in each case to the presence of both."

PHIL.   Fine! I grasp your view, except for a few points. For instance, why do you employ the method of isolation?

And what, more concretely, do you mean by the principle of organic unities?

MOORE. As regards the principle of isolation, by employing it, we shall guard against an error which appears to have been one of the chief causes that have vitiated previous conclusions on the subject. This error consists "in supposing that what seems absolutely necessary here and now, for the existence of anything good — what we cannot do without — is therefore good in itself. If we isolate such things, which are means to good, and suppose a world in which they alone, and nothing but they, existed, their intrinsic worthlessness becomes apparent." Now as far the principle of organic unities is concerned, I would say this. An organic unity, as I use the term, is a unity that has value different from the sum of the values of its parts. The principle of organic unities says that in considering the different *degrees* in which things themselves possess value, we have to take into account the fact that a whole may possess it in a degree different from that which is obtained by merely summing the degrees in which its parts possess it. Thus it warns us against the error or past moral philosophers who assumed that the value of a whole is the same as the sum of the values of its parts. It was by means of this conception that I was able to get beyond the point of view of Henry Sidgwick and Franz Brentano, with whom, as I said before, I have otherwise much in common. They seem to hold that the value of things is simply the sum of those elements into which they can be resolved by analysis. But this is clearly not so. Thus, take the case of an aesthetic enjoyment, or appreciation of a beautiful object. (Aesthetic enjoyments, I said, as you will recall, include some of the greatest intrinsic goods.) What are the main elements contained in such enjoyment? There is (1) some kind of feeling or emotion of appreciation and (2) a cognition of beautiful qualities. Each of these elements is equally essential; and each has equally little value by itself. But the *whole* in which both are combined as parts has a value greatly in excess of the sum of the values of its parts. Again, if there is added to this whole (3) a true belief in the reality of the object, the new whole thus formed has a value greatly in excess of the sum obtained by adding the value of the true belief, considered in itself, to that of our original whole. Does this answer your question?

PHIL.   It does, very adequately. But there are a few other points I would like to have explained. You spoke of 'great intrinsic evils.' What are these?

MOORE.   Great intrinsic evils consist in either (1) the love of what is evil or ugly, or in (2) the hatred of what is good or beautiful, or in (3) the consciousness of pain.

PHIL.   I see. And what about '*mixed* goods?' Do you recognize such things?

MOORE.   I certainly do. By 'mixed goods' I understand those goods which include some element of the evil or ugly. They consist either in hatred of the first two kinds of evil or ugliness, or in compassion for pain.

PHIL.   Very well. Then there is this question I would like to ask. You have made the distinction between 'good in itself' and 'good as a means.' The former you have explained. Would you please now explain the latter?

MOORE.   Yes, certainly. The question that you ask leads us into the third division of ethics. The first two we have, rather sketchily, covered. In the first part we dealt with the question: What is the nature of the predicate peculiar to ethics, namely, of 'good?' In the second part we discussed the question: What kinds of things themselves possess this predicate? In the third division we are concerned with the question: What is a means to good, what is the cause or necessary condition of things good in themselves? This is a question of *practical ethics.* It really is the question: "What ought we to do?" Or: "What actions are 'duties,' what actions are 'right' and what 'wrong?'" Now 'good as means' is any action which is either 'right' or 'useful,' or is a 'duty.' 'Right' means 'cause of good results,' and is thus identical with 'useful.' 'Duty,' on the other hand, can be defined as "that action which will bring the greatest possible amount of good in the Universe."

PHIL. If I remember correctly, you think that propositions with regard to duty are not self-evident. Thus, you would consider the intuitionism of Broad and Ross mistaken on this matter?

MOORE. Indeed. It seems to me that no proposition with regard to right or duty can be self-evident. I think that judgments about duty are capable of being confirmed or refuted by an investigation of causes and effects. Here I side with Brentano, in holding that this class of propositions *are* capable of proof or disproof and are not known intuitively. In fact, I think that there are so many different considerations relevant to the truth or falsehood of each such proposition, as to make the attainment of certainty impossible, and the attainment of probability very difficult. Still, the *kind* of evidence necessary and alone relevant to such proof and disproof can be exactly defined. It must contain propositions of two kinds only: (1) Causal truths; that is, truths with regard to the results of the action in question. (2) Ethical truths of our first or self-evident class — those asserting a connection between 'good' and a natural characteristic. It follows, that if any ethical philosopher fails to adduce *both* causal and ethical truths for

propositions about right or duty, or adduces for such propositions truths that are neither, his reasoning has not the least
tendency to establish his conclusions — his conclusions are
totally devoid of weight.

PHIL.   I am sorry to see that there is such a radical difference of view concerning our knowledge of propositions
about right or duty.

ROSS.   The difference, Philagathos, is not really as great
as at first sight appears. I think that if certain distinctions are
made, which Moore has not made, our positions will be seen
not to differ radically. In the first place, it is necessary to
distinguish between 'prima facie' duties and 'actual' or 'absolute'
duties. A 'prima facie' or 'conditional' duty is "the characteristic (quite distinct from that of being a duty proper) which
an act has, in virtue of being of a certain kind (for example, the
keeping of a promise), of being an act which would be a duty
proper if it were not at the same time of another kind which
is morally significant." Such duties may be classified as follows:
(1) *deontological* duties, such as fidelity, gratitude and justice,
(2) *teleological* duties, such as beneficence, self-improvement,
and non-malevolence. An 'actual' or 'absolute' duty, on the other
hand, is the duty to do one particular act in particular circum-
stances. Now prima facie duties are always *intuited* and certain,
while actual duties are *not* intuited — our knowledge of them
is always fallible. Thus, for instance, I intuitively and certainly know that promise-keeping is a duty; but in a particular
situation I cannot be sure that I ought to keep a promise or
do something else, for there are other ethical considerations
involved. Now it seems to me that when Moore said that no
moral law is self-evident he had been thinking only of *actual*
duties, and failed to distinguish these clearly from prima facie
or conditional duties. Thus, he says that "it is very improbable

and quite impossible to prove that any single action is *in all cases* better as means than its probable alternatives." I fully agree on this. But when he goes on and asserts that *"rules of duty*, even in this restricted sense, can only at most be general truths," I cannot agree. Further, he defines 'right' and 'ought' or 'duty' in terms of 'good.' This is because he lumps all duties together, and fails to make the important distinction between deontological and teleological duties. An act may be right not because it is conducive to good, but because it is itself the right production. This is true of the deontological duties. Thus, it is a mistake to hold that 'right' is always analyzable and definable as 'cause of a good result,' 'useful,' 'what is good as a means,' and the like; in short, that it can always be analyzed and defined in terms of good. It is *not* the case that 'right' does and can mean *nothing but* 'cause of a good result,' and thus is always identical with 'useful.' This is true only of some duties, those namely which I have called 'teleological.'

PHIL. I see now precisely where you and Moore differ and where you agree. Both views seems plausible. But if I were asked to cast a vote on this particular issue, I would probably decide to cast it in your favor, believing as I do in common sense — which, if I am right, regards our prima facie duties to be true — and being deeply impressed by theories of innate knowledge of ethical principles.

ROSS. I am glad to see that you are inclined to accept my view. But I must warn you that I am no Platonist. I do not think that we have these notions and this knowledge when we enter into the world, or that everybody attains it sooner or latter. I only believe that in the present stage of civilization most thoughtful and well-educated adults attain it.

PHIL. I understand your position. I would like to see

how Broad's compares with it.

BROAD.   I regret to say that I have not worked out my
view on this matter in a detailed way. But the conclusions
at which I have thus far arrived are quite in line with those
of Ross. I have already said that it seems to me almost certain that 'right' and 'ought' *cannot* be defined in terms of 'good,'
as Moore teaches; and also, that there *are* necessary propositions connecting these ethical characteristics with non-ethical
ones, and that these propositions can be seen to be necessary
by inspection. Again, I agree with Ross in not accepting the
doctrine of innate knowledge. Though I hold that our concepts
of ethical characteristics are *a priori* and not empirical, I think
that *reason forms* them; and that it would not form them unless *experience* provided suitable occasions, that is, the feelings
and emotions of approval and disapproval in certain situations.
As regards universal ethical propositions, these, I believe, are
never analytic. That is, I do not think that we start with a
knowledge of them before meeting with instances of them;
instead, I think they are *synthetic a priori*.

PHIL.   I see. But I must remark that *my a priorism* does
not deny a place to experience. Experience, I would say, *sug-
gests* the universal; reason needs experience as a kind of
stimulus for recovering its latent, unconscious knowledge. This
point, however, is a secondary matter here, so let us leave it
aside. I have now a pretty good idea of the views of all three
of you on 'right' and 'duty' and propositions involving these.
But with regard to 'the things that are intrinsically good' I have
not heard your view Broad, or yours, Ross.

BROAD.   Once more, I regret to say that I do not have
a worked out view. But I am prepared to accept the pluralistic
element in Moore's view. He makes the point that "very many

different things are good and evil in themselves, and . . . neither class of things possesses any other property which is *both common* to all its members *and peculiar* to them." In this I am almost certain he is right. I do not think, in other words, that there is any one non-ethical characteristic which is common and peculiar to everything that is intrinsically good. This means that I regard as mistaken the monistic theory of value, which asserts that there *is* a non-ethical characteristic which is both common and peculiar to all intrinsically good things. Thus, for instance, I regard as mistaken ethical hedonism, which considers pleasure as common and peculiar to all intrinsically good things, so that "all that is intrinsically good is pleasant, and all that is pleasant is intrinsically good."

PHIL.   A very interesting and important issue you have brought out, and one which I had almost wholly missed: pluralism vs. monism of value. It seems to me that ethical pluralism is right. But I wonder what Ross thinks.

ROSS.   I believe that the pluralistic theory of value is true, and have no criticism to advance against what Broad just said.

PHIL.   Tell us, then, how many kinds of intrinsically good things do you recognize?

ROSS.   I recognize four. These are (1) virtue, (2) knowledge, (3) pleasure, and (4) the apportionment of pleasure and pain to the virtuous and vicious, respectively.

PHIL.   You include knowledge in your list. Do you place it higher than pleasure?

ROSS.   Definitely. It seems clear to me that knowledge is better than pleasure, and the desire to know "is among the most salient elements of a good moral character."

PHIL. I think so, too. And do you place knowledge above or below virtue?

ROSS. Below. Moral goodness I consider infinitely superior to anything else.

PHIL. And how does moral goodness compare with pleasure?

ROSS. I consider pleasure far more inferior than knowledge. No amount of pleasure, however great, is equal in goodness to any amount of virtue, however small.

PHIL. I accept your hierarchy. However, your list of intrinsically good things does not seem to include the organic unities of which Moore spoke. Yet it appears that there is practically no good pleasure that is not part of a whole that is far better than the pleasure which it embraces.

ROSS. But "it seems at least arguable that the element other than pleasure, in the complex whole — the element of *insight* — has great intrinsic value, enough to account entirely for the superior value of the whole in which it is an element."

PHIL. Perhaps. And I would very much like to think that it has, for I love knowledge. There are other points which I would like to have cleared up somewhat in the remaining time we have at our disposal. You agree with Moore in admitting knowledge and pleasure among the intrinsically good things. But I don't know how the two of you compare in the matter of virtue and of the allocation of pain.

MOORE. You will recall that I divided positive evils into three classes. The first two are (1) evils which consist in the love, admiration, or enjoyment of what is evil or ugly; and (2) evils which consist in the hatred or contempt of what is good or beautiful. Now I think that when pain is added to these two states, the whole thus formed is always better, as a whole, than if no pain were there. "Whether such a state can constitute a positive good is another question."

PHIL.   Then you and Ross are in agreement here. Now as regards virtue, he considers it the greatest intrinsic good, while you rank aesthetic enjoyment and personal affection highest. How do you evaluate virtue?

MOORE.   Virtue generally has no value in itself. And where it has it is far from being the sole good or the best goods.

PHIL.   I do not quite grasp your meaning. Could you elaborate upon your view a bit?

MOORE.   Certainly. By virtue I mean mainly a permanent disposition to perform duties. Accordingly a virtue must be good as a *means*. Now a virtue, besides being good as a means, *may* also have intrinsic value. On the other hand, it may have none, as in the case of unconscious habits. But even where it has, it is far from being the only good — there are other goods. And further, it is never the best of goods.

PHIL.   I understand you better now. Your ideas on virtue clearly differ significantly from Ross'. You agree with him, however, in so far as you recognize intrinsic value in some virtues. I would like to know next which virtues you believe have intrinsic value and which do not.

MOORE.   In the first place, virtue that consists in the mere 'unconscious habit' of performing duties has *no* intrinsic value whatsoever, though it has value as a means. In the second place, where virtue consists in a disposition to have, and be moved by, a sentiment of *love* towards really *good* consequences of an action and of *hatred* towards really *evil* ones, it has *some* intrinsic value; but the value it has may vary greatly in degree. And in the third place, where virtue consists in *conscientiousness,* it seems to have *some* intrinsic value. Christianity has exaggerated the value of this feeling, while Kant erroneously thought that it was the sole thing of value. Now the two classes of virtue which have intrinsic value I classify with what I earlier called 'mixed goods.'

PHIL.   I think I have now a good understanding of your position with regard to virtue. But on this, as on most of the other questions that we have touched, I shall have to reflect a great deal more before I finally make up my mind. You, along with Ross and Broad, have clarified for me many of the issues of ethics; and for this I am extremely grateful to you. There are a number of other questions which I would have liked to discuss with you, but I do not dare to ask you to tarry much longer. I shall have to discuss them with you some other time. Yet there is one question which for me is pressing, and on which I would like to have you shed light.

MOORE.   What is that question?

PHIL.   It is this: Can ethics be unified and reduced to a system?

MOORE.   I think not.

PHIL.   What makes you say this?

MOORE.   Simply the facts. You no doubt have noticed that some of the attributions of intrinsic value, which seem to me to be true, do not display that symmetry which is wont to be required of philosophers. But if this be urged as an objection, I must respectfully point out that it is none. "To search for 'unity' and 'system' at the expense of truth, is not, I take it, the proper business of philosophy, however, universally it may have been the practice of philosophers. Of course, the study of ethics would be far more simple, and its results far more 'systematic,' if, for instance, pain were an evil of exactly the same magnitude as pleasure is a good; but we have no reason whatever to assume that the Universe is such that ethical truths must display this kind of symmetry: no argument against my conclusion, that pleasure and pain do *not* thus correspond, can have any weight whatever, failing a careful examination of the instances which have led me to form it."

PHIL.   You make a strong case against unity and system in ethics. And what is *your* view on this matter, Ross?

ROSS.   My view is similar to that of Moore. I see no *a priori* grounds for supposing that all good things are good for the same reason; or for supposing that all right acts are right for the same reason; or for supposing that there can be a 'general theory of value.' Truth is truth, beauty is beauty, and goodness is goodness; and we must not lump all these together. To repeat my friend Moore's quotation from Butler: "Everything is what it is and not another thing." In short, I find many irreducibles, which make it necessary to repress completely the desire for system in the interest of the desire for truth.

PHIL.   The words which you and Moore just uttered evince that both of you are true dialecticians, cutting up reality like Plato's model philosopher, "where the natural joints are and not trying to break any part, after the manner of the bad carver."[8] And now you, Broad, whose statements also plainly show that you belong to this group, please shed one final ray of light on this subject. From what you have said thus far, I am sure that you are no less hostile to attempts at unity and system in ethics.

BROAD. That is true. You recall that I find many irreducibles, just as Ross does. I do *not* think that all self-evident
principles of ethics can be brought under any *one* supreme
principle. All attempts to do so oversimplify the actual situation. Again, the study of ethics shows that the subject of human
desire, emotion, and action is extremely complex; rendered so
by the paradoxical position of man, half-animal and half-angel,
completely at home in none of the mansions of his Father's
house, — too refined to like to behave as an animal and too
coarse to live as an angel.

THREE TALKS
WITH G. E. MOORE

THREE TALKS WITH G. E. MOORE

FIRST TALK

I met Moore and his wife for the first time in the afternoon of December 20, 1947. The meeting took place in their home at 86 Chesterton Road, Cambridge. I had written to Moore days in advance, and he invited me to visit him on this date at 5:00 in the afternoon.

When I arrived at their home, I rang the door bell and waited. Soon, a short, stooped, white-haired, spectacled man opened the door. It was Moore. He greeted me with a smile and a very strong handshake, and led me to his study. There we sat down opposite an electrically heated fireplace.

Moore asked me where I was living, and how long I planned to stay in Cambridge. The conversation turned briefly to conditions in Greece and France, where I sojourned before I came to England. While I conveyed to him my impressions, he listened with apparent interest, but said little. In connection with the philosophy in those countries, I mentioned my visiting in Greece several academic philosophers, in particular Voreas, Theodorakopoulos, Imvriotis and Theodoridis, and auditing in France some of the lectures of Souriau, Bachelard, Bayer, and Schuhl.

41

Next, Moore asked me with whom I had been doing work at Harvard. I mentioned Ralph Barton Perry, C. I. Lewis, Raphael Demos, John Wild, and Donald C. Williams. He showed special interest in Perry.

Assuming the initiative in the conversation, I asked Moore what he taught before retiring. He replied:

"At first, I taught for several years Psychology, mainly Philosophical Psychology. I mean such stuff as Stout deals with in his *Analytic Psychology* and *A Manual of Psychology*, and William James in his *Principles of Psychology.* I did not deal with experimental psychology. Then I taught, in addition, Metaphysics. From 1925 I taught only Metaphysics."

"What system of teaching did you follow?" I asked.

"My system was to lecture for an hour, and then to have immediately follow a discussion for another hour. It worked very well. However, teaching for two successive hours tires one; and at the end of the session I felt exhausted."

"What was the size of your classes?"

"Classes in philosophy at Cambridge University are generally of not more than twelve students. I think that in philosophy it is important to have discussion, and hence a small number of students."

"I fully agree," I remarked.

Then I asked Moore something about his article "Identity," which appeared in the *Proceedings of the Aristotelian Society* at the turn of the century.[1] I read it recently, as relevant to the topic of my Ph.D. dissertation, *The Classical Theory of Relations.* Moore had no desire to discuss his article.

"Don't you think it is terribly confused?" he asked.

"I think there are some confusions in it," I replied. "But I would not say it is *terribly* confused!"

"Oh, yes, yes!" he said. "It's awful! I didn't know what I was saying there!"

In connection with the subject of relations, Moore told me that he was surprised when he read in my letter that I was writing on Plato's and Aristotle's theory of relations, for he was of the opinion that they did not have such a theory or even a term for relation. To this, I replied that Plato used for relation the term *pros allon*, 'towards another,' while Aristotle employed *pros ti*, 'towards something;' and that they both have much to say about relations.[2]

In our discussion of relations, the distinction between 'essential' and 'accidental' came up. I spoke of 'essential relations' and 'accidental relations' (or what he and others call 'internal relations' and external relations'), and said that I found this distinction in the ancients. Moore remarked that the distinction between 'essential' and 'accidental' is never explained by the ancients. Then, he added that they failed to draw the distinction between the essence of *man* and the essence of *Socrates*, i.e the individual. I did not argue with him on these points, but let him instead proceed to explain the distinction between essential and accidental as he understood it.

Moore defined 'essential' as that which *entails* such and such other characteristics. In the case of accidental characteristics there is no such entailment. With regard to the *essence* of *man*, Moore said that this consists of a few characteristics, such that if one does not have them we reject him right off as clearly not being a man. Within essence there are, he said, *no degrees*.

Plato, Aristotle and Aquinas, hold that a relation *belongs to* a thing. For instance, in the relational situation "Simmias is taller than Socrates," the relation 'taller than' holds from Simmias to Socrates, but inheres (in an unique and indefinable way) only in Simmias. Moore holds that a relation belongs neither to the referent (in this case Simmias) nor to the relatum (Socrates). It is a 'relational property,' as distinct from the relation, that belongs to the referent, and another 'relational property' that belongs to the relatum. A relational property, says Moore, is the property of standing in a particular relation.

When our conversation had reached the one and a half hour mark, Moore's wife came in and interrupted us. She explained to me that she did this in order to safeguard his health. He had a heart attack the previous year, she said, and the physician warned him to stop lecturing altogether, so as not to tire himself. Mrs. Moore seems much younger than her seventy-four year old husband.

Moore offered me cigarettes. I thanked him, and explained that I did not smoke. He himself did not smoke cigarettes, but a pipe. He fiddled with it from the time I entered the house, filled it with tobacco once or twice, but produced very little smoke.

During the meeting, I took note of the following traits of Moore. He listens intently, grasps very easily what you want to say, and is ready to start off answering in his habitual analytical way. He speaks as he writes, frequently emphasizing certain words. He is very humane, having a warmth that is rare among philosophers. When the conversation is non-philosophical, he is relaxed and genial. But he becomes transformed when the discussion is philosophical. He becomes tense, his features, particularly his extraordinarily bright and penetrating eyes, assume the expression of a nervous critic. A phrase he tends to use when he is about to set out to clear up a difficult point is: "Look here!" When he is through, he is wont to ask: "Do you see it now? Do you see it?"

SECOND TALK

My second conference with Moore took place two days after Christmas, at the same time as the previous one, between 5:00 and 6:30. On this occasion, we discussed particularly his articles "The Refutation of Idealism," which was published in Volume 12 (1903) of *Mind*, and "External and Internal Relations," which appeared in Volume 20 (1919-1920) of the *Proceedings of the Aristotelian Society*. I asked Moore if he still abided by what he had said in his "Refutation of Idealism." He replied thus:

"There are a number of things in my 'Refutation' which are wrong. I attributed to Berkeley the view that the being of *every* entity is *percipi* (being perceived). But Berkeley does not say this. *Only* in the case of *'ideas'* does he say that the being of a thing is *percipi*. I see that I cannot refute *this*; and I am not sure that Berkeley was wrong in asserting it. If you arrange sensations ('ideas') along a scale, from a sensation of *blue* to a sensation of *pain,* you can start from blue and proceed to the other end and argue that pain exists independently of being perceived. But if you start from pain — which I think *cannot* exist without being perceived — and move towards the other end, then blue becomes dependent on being perceived."

"What is the *referent* in sensation?" I asked.

"The *ego*," he replied. "The ego is *spatial,* in the sense of occupying a *position,* but *not* in the sense of being extended.

Locke remarked that when he left one city and went to another he took his mind with him. The ego, the mind, is for me *real*. I do not seek to reduce it to something else. Russell has proposed an alternative view of mind, that of neutral monism. But I have not been able to work out such a theory; and my own view seems adequate to me."

"It seems adequate to me also," I remarked. "It is simpler and more reasonable."

"I think so."

"Now what about the *object,* when one is aware of it? Does it change at all by entering into relation with a mind?" I asked.

"The object, when I am aware of it, does gain a relational property. But the thing nevertheless remains the *same, precisely* the same. This is because the *nature* of a thing consists of its *intrinsic* attributes. We don't — unless we are philosophers with a particular bias — speak of a thing as *changing* when it gains or loses relational properties. We just *don't.*"

"What about our *knowledge of relations?*" I asked next. "Do we *see* the relation 'above' in the case of two books, for instance, or is there a *judgment* involved?"

"There is no judgment. We *see* the relation. But *seeing* here is used in a very different sense from seeing the *color* of a book, or seeing the *interval* between them. William James wrongly supposed that the *spatial interval* between two things was a relation. In the case of the relation 'above,' I see *that* one thing is above the other."

"The *place* a thing occupies," Moore went on to say, "is *not* a relation. A thing *has* a relation to a place; but the place *is not* the relation. It's absurd to identify them."

What especially struck me about his philosophy, as it came through in these discussions, was the lack of a comprehensive world view. He makes analysis upon analysis, distinction after distinction. But he makes no effort to interrelate the results of his analyses and distinctions, so as to give you a somewhat unified vision of man and the universe.

During this conference, as during the previous one, I was impressed by the affection Moore displayed. He takes interest in one as a person. He asked how I liked Garden House Hotel, where I am staying, how I was enjoying my stay in Cambridge, and so on.

As I was about to leave, I thanked him for helping me understand better a number of things in his philosophy. This seemed to please him.

THIRD TALK

On January 20, 1948, I met Moore for the third and last time. We met earlier for this conference, at 2:30, and talked until 4:00. The weather was colder than on the other occasions. Moore wore his overcoat, and we both sat near the hearth. It had snowed, and we talked about the snow. But soon we turned to philosophical questions.

I asked Moore about his article in Baldwin's *Dictionary of Philosophy* on "Relative." He said he had forgotten it, did not remember a thing of what he said there. I read to him this statement, which I had copied in my notebook:

"As applied to things, 'relative' is never merely synonymous with 'related;' it is always distinguished therefrom by implying that the relation or relations to which it refers are *essential* to the subject of which it is predicated, i.e. that this subject is one which can only be defined by some property such as might be expressed by a relative term."[3]

"Everything which has a relation or relations," I observed, "is relative to the thing or things to which it is related; but these relations are *not necessarily essential* to it."

"I agree," said Moore. "I was then confused, as we often are, between what a thing is as related (e.g. father), and what a thing is apart from the relation (e.g. man)."

"Next I read a passage from his *Philosophical Studies*:

"I conceive, observation might justify us in concluding that certain kinds of things — pains, for example, do *not* exist, when they are not perceived and that other kinds of things — colours, for example, *do* exist, when they are not perceived."[4]

"Do you now think there *are* observations which *can* prove these propositions?" I asked Moore.

"I know of none," he replied. "They could be proved only by some *a priori* principle or principles that are either self-evident or plausible."

This admission, together with the one made in the Second Talk, in connection with George Berkeley, made me realize that Moore's 'refutation of idealism' was not so well-grounded as many have supposed.

Next, we turned to subjects which are central in perennial philosophy: God, immortality, and the mind-body relationship. I knew from his writings that Moore has professed to be an agnostic on the first two questions. But I thought now in his old age he might have adopted some kind of affirmative position. I remarked that, so far as I knew, he had not dealt with these questions. He told me that he had dealt with them in his paper "A Defense of Common Sense,"[5] which was first published in 1925,[6] and in his review of H. Cornelius' book *Einleitung in die Philosophie* which appeared in 1905.[7]

"As regards God," he explained, "I think that all the traditional arguments are unsound; and I don't know of any way of proving God. As far as immortality is concerned, I don't know of any possible way of proving it, either, except experimentally, by science — for example, by Psychical Research. Broad has adopted this approach, and I believe it is the right one."

The question about the mind-body, or soul-body, relationship was somehow left unanswered. Moore said nothing about it, and we did not come back to it. In his "A Defense of Common Sense" and his review of Cornelius' book, to which Moore referred me, I have not found a discussion of this subject. What I have found in the review is a strong affirmation of the reality of a plurality of minds, with which I fully agree. Moore submits:

"It is plain . . . that the existence of a plurality of minds must be at least as certain as any theory about the nature of *our* knowledge. Any theory of knowledge which casts a doubt upon our knowledge of the existence of other minds, thereby destroys its own credit. . . . Our knowledge that other minds exist is at least as certain as our knowledge that *we* know our own perceptions."[8]

I had intended all along to ask Moore some questions pertaining to his ethical philosophy, about which he is best known. The opportunity presented itself at this point. I asked him about "non-natural" characters, as defined in his *Principia Ethica,* saying that I was troubled by this distinction.

"My way of distinguishing non-natural characteristics, in *Principia Ethica*," said Moore, "is all wrong. Broad's answer in the Schilpp volume[9] is one way of distinguishing them. My own way, in this same volume, is another way. Both are good, and the two ways are not incompatible with one another."

"How do we become aware of, or know, goodness?" I asked.

"To this I have no answer. I am content to assert *that* we apprehend goodness, even though I cannot explain *how* we apprehend it."

"Do you still hold that goodness is indefinable?"

"I now think that it can be defined with reference to *ought*. You start from 'better.' You 'ought' to do what is 'better.' From 'better' you get to what is *intrinsically* good. The *relation* of ought, of duty, to good is *internal*."

Finally, I asked Moore this question:

"What authors, and what works of theirs, do you consider as the most important for one's acquiring a good grounding in philosophy?" In asking this, I was prompted by the desire to learn more definitely his character as a philosopher, in accordance with the saying: "Show me your books and I will show you who you are."

"That is a very big question!" he said. Then, pausing briefly, he began making suggestions, as follows:

"Of English writers, I would recommend F. P. Ramsey, Wittgenstein, W. E. Johnson, and Russell. Ramsey's book *The Foundations of Mathematics and Other Logical Essays* is very good, even though later parts sometimes contradict earlier ones. It is a very suggestive work. The *Tractatus Logico-Philosophi-*

cus of Wittgenstein is very enlightening. As far as Johnson is concerned, I would recommend especially the first volume of his *Logic*. There is much in this work with which I disagree; but there is also much that I find excellent. Russell's Introduction to *Principia Mathematica* is the greatest thing he has written. His *Introduction to Mathematical Philosophy* is good, though it repeats the Introduction to *Principia*. I would not recommend his *Principles of Mathematics*; it is very confused and full of mistakes.

"Of Germans, I think that Brentano and Meinong are especially worth studying. Brentano's writings are excellent, particularly his *Psychologie*. He has an excellent approach, is clear and profound. But he sometimes makes mistakes on simple points. His pupil Meinong is very clear and acute, especially in his *Üeber Annahmen*.

"As far as the French are concerned, Nicod and Poincaré stand out in my estimation. I would recommend Nicod's *Le Problème logique de l'induction* and *La Géométrie dans le monde sensible*, and Poincaré's *La Science et l'hypothèse*.

Surprised that he did not mention Meyerson and Bergson, I asked Moore what he thought of them. He said:

"Meyerson and Bergson are second-raters. Meyerson is often confused, while Bergson is always confused. Bergson hasn't written anything that is clear, though he has a beautiful style."

Turning, finally, to American philosophers, Moore singled out William James and Alfred North Whitehead.

"James and Whitehead," he said, "are the greatest of the American philosophers.*The Principles of Psychology* is James' best work. Not because his answers are always sound, but because of his *approach* and his *acute criticism* of the views of others. Whitehead's best works are his earlier ones, most notably *The Concept of Nature*. In *Process and Reality,* which appeared later, there is much confusion. The confusion is not due to the fact that the ideas are difficult, but to the fact that Whitehead's *thinking them out* was confused."

It became evident from Moore's reply to my question that what he prizes above all in philosophical works are sheer clarity, acuteness, and the absence of inconsistencies. He stands in sharp contrast in this respect with philosophers such as Bergson and Whitehead, who emphasize above all intuition or insight that grasps ultimate truths and gives man a profound and unifying vision of the totality of things, material and spiritual.

I thanked Moore for this and the other two opportunities he gave me of meeting him and discussing a wide variety of philosophical questions.

Before bidding him and his gracious wife good-bye, I asked him to autograph his *Ethics*, which I had purchased at one of the bookstores in Cambridge. This he gladly did.

About this work, Moore says in his autobiography: "My small book called *Ethics* I myself like better than *Principia Ethica,* because it seems to me to be much clearer and far less full of confusions and invalid arguments."[10]

NOTES

A DIALOGUE ON
G. E. MOORE'S ETHICAL PHILOSOPHY

1 'Lover (*philos*) of goodness or the good (*agathon*).'

2 W. D. Ross, *The Right and the Good*, p. 13.

3 Cf. G. E. Moore, *Principia Ethica*, pp. 6-7: "Definitions of the kind that I was asking for, definitions which describe the real nature of the object or notion denoted by the word, and which do not merely tell us what the word is used to mean, are only possible when the object or notion in question is something complex. You can give a definition of a horse, because a horse has many different properties and qualities, all of which you can enumerate. But when you have reduced a horse to his simplest terms, then you can no longer define these terms."

4 In a conversation I had with Moore in January, 1948, at his home in Cambridge, he expressed a change of attitude as regards the indefinability of good. He remarked that he now thought good *could* be defined by relating it to duty. There is, he said, an *internal* relationship between duty and good.

5 D. C. Williams, "The Meaning of 'Good,'" *The Philosophical Review*, July, 1937, p. 418.

6 During the conversation mentioned in note 4, Moore admitted that this way of defining 'non-natural' characteristics in *Principia Ethica* "was all wrong." He added that Broad's way of distinguishing 'non-natural' from 'natural' characteristics, as it appears in Paul A. Schilpp's volume *The Philosophy of G. E. Moore*, is a good way of distinguishing them, and so also is his own way in the same volume. Moore went on to say that the two ways are not incompatible with one another.

[7] Even as late as the time when I met him, in 1948, Moore had no answer to offer to the question of how he believed we become aware of, or know, goodness.

[8] *Phaedrus* 265e

THREE TALKS WITH G. E. MOORE

[1] Vol. 1 (1900-1901), pp. 103-127.

[2] See my book *The Classical Theory of Relations,* Belmont, Mass., 1975.

[3] Vol. 2 (1902), p. 443.

[4] London, 1922, pp. 91-92.

[5] Moore does not really discuss these questions in "A Defense of Common Sense." He has only a brief paragraph on God, and a briefer one on the after-life, in which he simply rejects dogmatically all arguments for God and immortality. (See his *Philosophical Papers,* New York, 1962, 1966, p. 52.) And he says nothing regarding the mind-body relationship. In his review of Cornelius' book there is nothing about God, immortality, or the mind-body relationship. But in his work *Some Main Problems of Philosophy,* which was published five years after this conference, Moore discusses all three questions. About God and the future life he does not have much to say: his discussion is confined to pp. 17-18. Here he asserts that "On the whole, it is fairest to say that Common Sense has *no* view on the question whether we do know that there is a God or not: that it neither asserts that we do know this nor yet that we do not;" and similarly that "It is perhaps fairest to say that Common Sense . . . asserts neither that we *do* know of a future life nor that we do *not.*" By a future life he understands this: "that besides the acts of consciousness attached to our bodies, while they are alive upon the earth, our minds go on performing acts of consciousness *not* attached to any living body on the surface of the earth." He goes on to say that both beliefs "go *beyond* the views of Common Sense," and that each certainly "is a most important addition" to what Common Sense believes about the Universe. Moore says, further, that although important additions to Common Sense, these beliefs "do not contradict it." As to why the belief in God is important, he has this to

say: "By a God is meant something so different both from material objects and from our minds, that to add that, besides these, there is also a God, is certainly to make an important addition to our view of the Universe;" while about the importance of the belief in a future life, he remarks: "If there really are going on in the Universe at this moment, not only the acts of consciousness attached to the living bodies of men and animals on the surface of this earth, but also acts of consciousness performed by the minds of millions of men, whose bodies have long been dead — then certainly the Universe is a very different place from what it would be, if this were not the case."

In *Some Main Problems of Philosophy* Moore also discusses the mind-body problem, in particular the "Interactionist" view, and devotes half a dozen pages (158-163) to it. He explains the interactionist view, examines two arguments which are commonly used against this view, and concludes that both arguments to prove that our minds and bodies could not possibly interact are inconclusive. He adds that he knows no better arguments to prove this; and that according to Common Sense, which he espouses, it is a "fact that our minds and bodies do interact" (p. 163).

6 In *Contemporary British Philosophy*, edited by J. H. Muirhead.

7 Published in *Mind*, n.s., Vol. 14, pp. 244-253.

8 *Op. cit.*, p. 252.

9 Paul Arthur Schilpp, editor, *The Philosophy of G. E. Moore*, Evanston and Chicago, 1942.

10 *Ibid.*, p. 27.

BIBLIOGRAPHY

Broad, C. D., *Five Types of Ethical Theory,* New York, 1930.

Moore, G. E., "Identity," *Proceedings of the Aristotelian Society,* Vol. 1 (1900-1901), pp. 103-127.

———— "Relative," *A Dictionary of Philosophy,* edited by J. M. Baldwin, Vol. 2, New York and London, 1902, pp. 443-446.

———— "The Refutation of Idealism," *Mind,* n.s., Vol. 12 (1903), pp. 433-453.

———— Review of *Einleitung in die Philosophie* by H. Cornelius, *Mind,* Vol. 14 (1905), pp. 244-253.

———— "External and Internal Relations," *Proceedings of the Aristotelian Society,* Vol. 20 (1919-1920), pp. 40-62. *Philosophical Studies,* 1922, pp. 276-309.

———— *Principia Ethica,* Cambridge, (Eng.), 1929 (1st ed. 1903).

———— *Ethics,* London, 1947 (1st ed. 1912).

———— *Philosophical Studies,* London, 1922.

———— "A Defense of Common Sense," *Contemporary British Philosophy,* edited by J. H. Muirhead, London, 1925. Also in *Philosophical Papers,* New York, 1962, 1966.

57

———— *Some Main Problems of Philosophy*, London, 1953.

Ross, W. D., *The Right and the Good*, Oxford, 1930.

Schilpp, Paul A., editor, *The Philosophy of G. E. Moore*, Vol. IV of *The Library of Living Philosophers*, Evanston and Chicago, 1942.

INDEXES

INDEX OF NAMES

INDEX OF SUBJECTS